Dragons of Moon Tail Island

Omar's Book of Dragons

Written by Miranda Walker
Illustrated by Lisa Hunt

Contents

Welcome to Moon Tail Island

Moon Tail Island is a very special island. The only way to get there is to fly … by dragon!

Read on to find out everything I've learned about the dragons who live there.

volcano

mountains

Sharp Tooth Bay

forest

caves

lake

My map of Moon Tail Island

Most humans can't see dragons. You can only see them if you truly believe in them.

There are nine types of dragons on Moon Tail Island.

fire dragons

cloud dragons

forest dragons

lake dragons

sand dragons

ice dragons

sea dragons

field dragons

mountain dragons

Fire dragons

Here's Ember. She is a fire dragon, although she doesn't breathe fire very often.

She likes learning about the human world.

Ember's cave is full of things she has collected. The things humans throw away is like treasure to her!

How many **groups** of different things does Ember have?
How many things are in each **group**?

Ember likes to organize her treasures. Whenever she brings home new things, she **tallies** them in a chart.

Treasure	Tally
bike wheels	||
buttons	𝍸 𝍸 𝍸 |
bolts	𝍸 ||||
shells	𝍸 𝍸

Look at Ember's **tally chart**. Which item does she have the **most** of? Which item does she have the **fewest** of?

Cloud dragons

Here's Nimbus. He's a cloud dragon.
Cloud dragons love to fly.

Nimbus is one of the fastest dragons on the island.

The cloud dragons keep the island hidden. They make sure it's surrounded by clouds.

Nimbus knows lots of different moves.

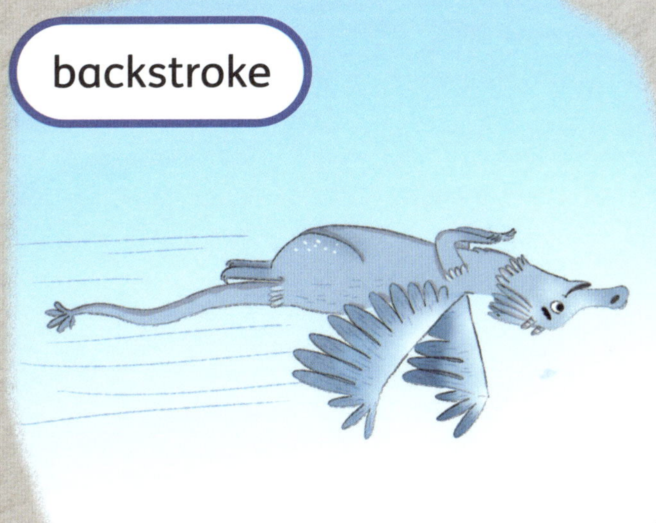

I kept a tally of Nimbus's moves during one flight.

Move	Tally
loop	卌 卌 ||
dive	||||
backstroke	卌 |
hover	卌 卌 卌

Look at Omar's **tally chart**. Which move did Nimbus do the **most**? Which move did he do the **least**?

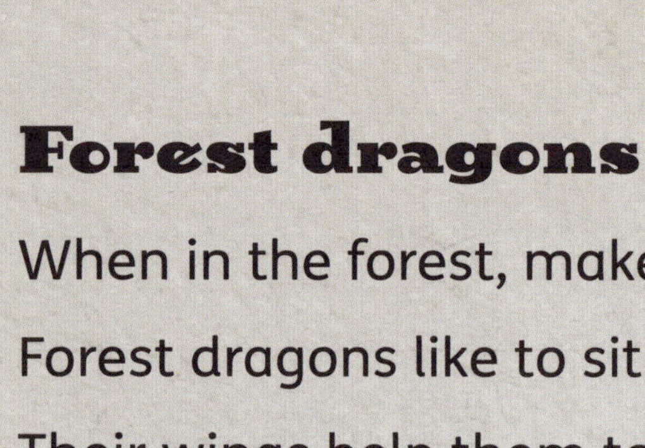

Forest dragons

When in the forest, make sure to look above you. Forest dragons like to sit high up on branches. Their wings help them to glide from tree to tree.

Forest dragons are the smallest of all the dragons.

Omar is counting the number of forest dragons. How do you think he should record the number of dragons he sees?

In the summer, forest dragons enjoy the shade of the leaves.

Forest dragons like to eat fruit that grows on the trees. Their favourite is flamefruit. It's similar to an apple but tastes spicy!

Lake dragons

Here's Trogo. He is a lake dragon.

Lake dragons are calm, wise dragons.
They love to read.

Trogo runs a library for all the dragons on the island to use.

Cave Library

Trogo

Lake dragons also like to sail. Sometimes they sail and read at the same time!

Dragons enjoy visiting the library.

There is even a book about humans! It can be found on the 'fiction' shelf.

Books borrowed	Tally	Total
4 or **more** books	|	1
2–3 books	𝍸	5
1 book	?	?

Look at the picture of the dragons borrowing books. What information is missing from the **tally chart**?

Sand dragons

Sand dragons live in Sharp Tooth Bay.

Instead of pebbles, there are jewels everywhere. They would be treasure in the human world, but dragons don't have much use for them.

Here's how many jewels I spotted during one visit:

Jewel	Total
diamonds	20
rubies	17
jade stones	10
pearls	13

Groups of jewels like this are found all over Sharp Tooth Bay!

Look at Omar's **table**. Omar said, 'There are **fewer** jade stones than rubies.' Is he correct?

Sand dragons build beautiful sandcastles. Their sandcastles are big enough to go inside.

Sand dragon sandcastles are very strong.

Here's a **table** about a sandcastle I visited:

Sandcastle feature	Total
windows	20
towers	7
flags	3

Omar has made a mistake in his **table**! Which number has he got wrong?

Ice dragons

Meet the ice dragons.

They live on the cold tip of the island, close to the mountains.

Their dens are made from ice, like igloos.

The furniture inside their dens is made from ice, too!

I'm not sure I'd want a bed or chair made from ice!

Ice dragons are very good ice skaters.

Other dragons come from all over the island, just to watch them skate.

Omar is counting the number of dragons on the ice.
How could he record the information?

Sea dragons

Moon Tail Island is surrounded by sea!

Sea dragons love to swim around all day.

They can hold their breath underwater for over an hour at a time.

Sea dragons have an important job.

They teach all the other dragons how to swim when they are young. Every dragon is then safe in the water.

Omar is recording the number of sea dragons that swim past him. He thinks a **tally chart** would be best. Do you agree?

Field dragons

Field dragons can be found in wide open fields.

They are a bit like farmers in the human world. They grow lots of different food for dragons to eat.

They use their wings to shelter plants from too much sun or rain.

The most popular fruit on Moon Tail Island is the moonberry.

There are three different kinds of moonberry.

Kind of moonberry	Tally
spotty	𝍸 𝍸 𝍸 𝍷
stripy	?
plain	𝍸 𝍸

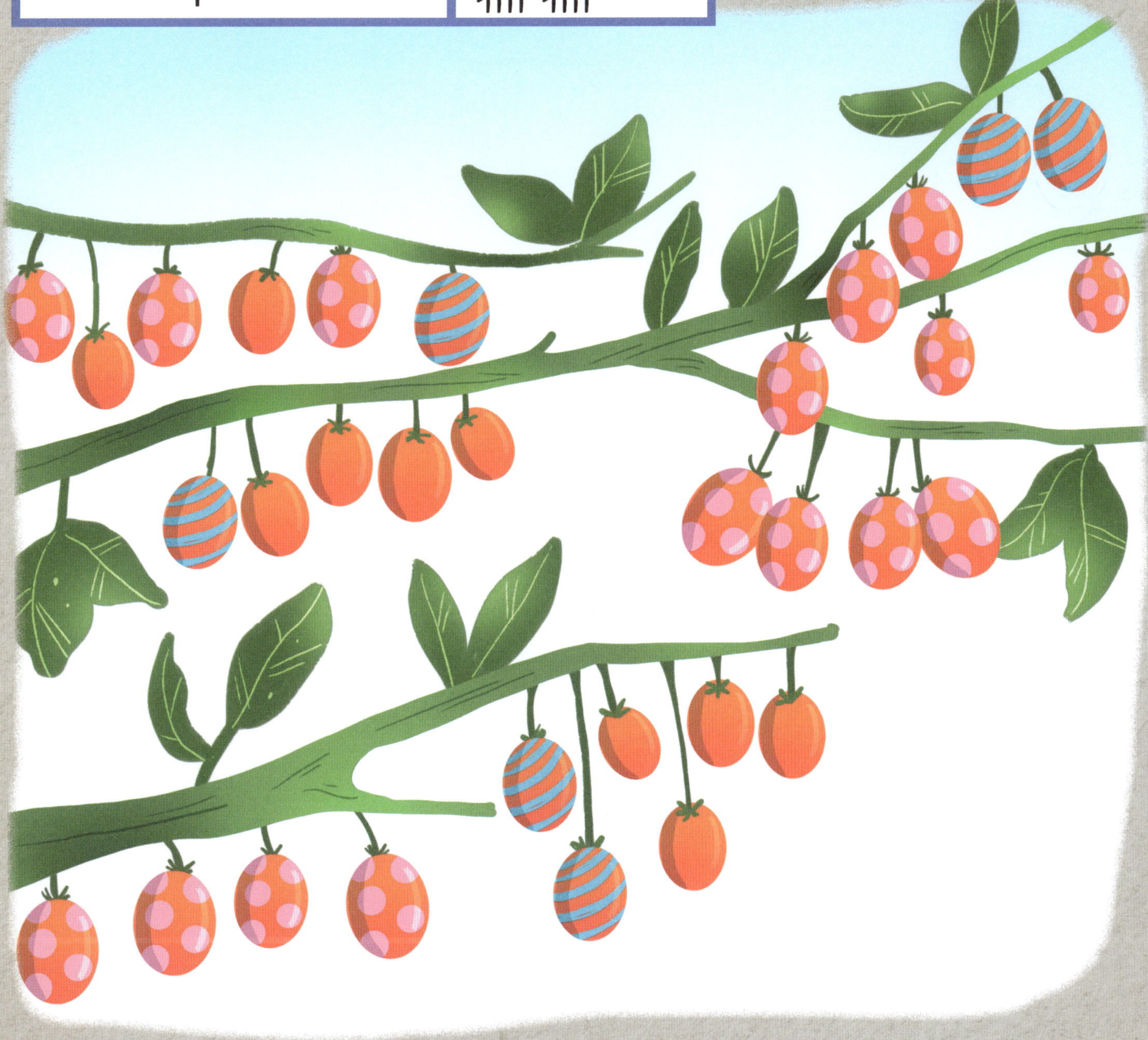

There are 6 stripy moonberries. How would you write 6 in **tally marks**?

Mountain dragons

Mountain dragons live high up. They like to fly around the mountaintops.

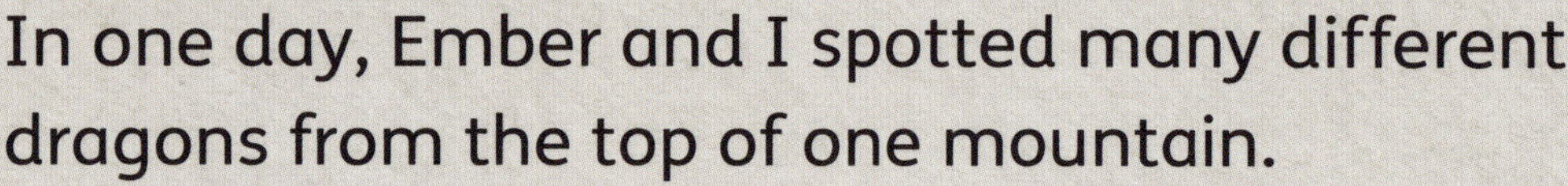

In one day, Ember and I spotted many different dragons from the top of one mountain.

Type of dragon	Tally	Total
fire dragon	𝍷	1
forest dragon	𝍸 𝍸 𝍸 𝍸 𝍷	21
field dragon	𝍸 𝍷𝍷𝍷𝍷	10
mountain dragon	𝍸 𝍸 𝍷𝍷𝍷𝍷	14

Look at the '**Tally**' column. Now look at the 'Total' column. Has Omar recorded the information correctly?

Mountain dragons are great climbers. They are also brilliant artists. They draw the beautiful views they can see from the top of the mountains.

The volcano

In the centre of the island there is a volcano.

Although it releases steam from time to time, it's perfectly safe. My sister and I flew over it in a dragon race!

Night of the Purple Moon

Every year, for one night, the moon turns purple. A special, beautiful flower blooms during that time.

To celebrate, all the dragons have a big party.

Dragon counting

Nadia and Omar decided to **tally** how many dragons they saw on a visit to Moon Tail Island.

1. Nadia saw 17 dragons.
Is her **tally** correct?

2. Omar saw 12 dragons.
How could he improve his **tally marks**?

Answers

p4. 4 groups – 10 shells, 16 buttons, 9 bolts, 2 bike wheels; p5. buttons (most), bike wheels (fewest); p7. Nimbus hovered the most (15 times) and dived the least (4 times); p8. a tally chart; p11. ||, 2; p12. yes; p13. There are 17 windows, not 20; p15. a tally chart; p17. yes; p19. 𝍸 |; p20. No, for field dragons the tally (9) does not match the total (10); p24. 1. No – Nadia's tally recorded 16 dragons, 2. Omar is correct, but he needs to use gates of five, 𝍸 𝍸 ||.